BOOK OF SHADOWS

Published by Dreaming Deer Press
Marietta, GA, USA 30067

Copyright © 2018 by Joseph S. Plum
All rights reserved.

ISBN-13: 9780692636398

ISBN-10: 0692636390

No portion of this book may be reproduced without prior written permission from the publisher, except brief selections for reviews or articles.

Cover art by Emily Lupita, watercolor & ink, 2004.

Printed in the United States of America

> For poetry books, CDs & DVDs
> by Joseph S. Plum, please visit:
>
> www.JoePlum.com

Book of Shadows

Joseph S. Plum

Preface

The poems written in this book were transcribed from the original oral poetry that was crafted in the bardic tradition of dreaming and living a lifetime in connection with nature. The hope is that by writing down the poems and collecting them into books, they may travel widely and be shared with the world. If you have a chance, please say these poems aloud. In this way, the beauty and power of traditional bardic poetry will live on through your voice.

Artist's Statement

    angels sleeping

    beyond the blue

    awaken

    as they tumble through!

              -Joseph Samuel Plum
                     from *blink*

Contents

royal companion 1

vibrations 7

solstice 15

sound of the living water 19

runaway 31

driving force 33

Aerion Cenote 37

falling 63

starlord 65

karmic pool 67

bowsong 71

out lined 75

for Earth

royal companion

in winter
fire is a royal companion
born out of kinship from old
where lifetime after lifetime,
wrapped in a robe of darkness,
a dreamer's destiny
takes years to unfold
until up from the lowest seat
of high position,
clear to the noble head
of a living throne,
there flames a procession
of bright intuition
burning with compassion,
elements
from the wandering unknown.
in the north a star has risen
beyond the sight of mortal men
while in the space and time that's given,
from inside,
a storm cloud approaching

signals the beginning
of the middle of the end.
    many children like to play with fire
though few have ever learned
how to grasp a life of passionate desire
without first getting their fingers burned.
who can sense an open doorway
when in blindness hands are busy passing on?
better still to be still
and enter in the timeless byways
where the warmth within leads
into a greater light beyond.
    across the battle ramparts,
the shining ones came from afar
to rest upon the wind-stilled waves,
disguised as the shimmering of a star.
if you seek to join
with the vanishing rays
of a living sun at twilight
as darkness begins again
to retake the sky,
travel now
beyond the boundaries

long ago established

by too much use of either i.

    while passing over the portals

each life spans the abyss,

opening and closing with memories

our bodies begin to believe

in a tune filled with sorrow and bliss.

for laid upon our bones is a rhythm

of muscle and fiber entwined in slumber,

a dreamsong

whose singers sleep down under

this blanket of flesh

and that covering of stars

without number

until in the fullness of time,

awakened by pure light

washing the mind,

the guardian of total harmony

begins to appear,

first by sucking silence

out of the inner ear,

then by creating chaos

for anyone near.

    if you begin to believe

these words that you hear,

know now

the edge of this world

can be very near,

    dragons in the dark

and deserts in the air

follow each other,

one by one,

until you thirst for breath

and burn from fear,

until quite suddenly,

with notice to none,

you just simply disappear.

    and so it is

that the song remains

long after the singer is gone.

    and so it is

the dream's unchanged

even though the dreamer awakes

to move on.

    and so it is
that the fire leaps
from the flame
to claim the hearts
of those who would do wrong.
and so it is
that when the new day comes
there are few of us left
to greet the dawn
and so it is
that fire is a royal companion
born out of kinship from old.

vibrations

    beside myself
i see a fool,
a ghost,
a spirit-being
who looks
a lot like me
and when we stand
so very still
what once was one
then became two
now turns again to three
for if by chance
our shadows cross
and the earth
is forced to compromise
from the very depths
of where light
and dark are one
a cascading sense of self
begins again to rise
    vibrations

of an ancient spirit

ancestral fiber

of the tribes

enters skillfully

by way of my feet

and flows

upward

out my eyes

in the grasp

of every waking moment

undoubtedly left

by those who sent us

to be offered up

in the speech

of the ones

who know it

is a hidden pathway

built of steps

well worth the learning

each one an open gateway

of non-returning

   when i was a child

and first entered into

this world of becoming

i drew down from the stars

a true sense of belonging

fathered by the light

of a great day in the morning

i grew strong through the process

of the old gods fulfilling

a promise to us

their children of the dawning

fostered

by the night wind's commitment

i reached the age of reason

and passed right on through it

until the day came

when i was ten

and there

for the benefit of those gods

i conducted that wind

into harmony

    as liquid darkness poured in

i learned

that borderline poetry

was to be sunk

into a wellspring of time

buried

in a casket of rhyme

    when i was ten

cedar root caves held stones

which would bleed

at my touch

and then my legs

would not stand

my mouth

would not speak

my mind would not recall

this world

or this world's sun

eyes

that once were mine

would return with time

to fix themselves

upon the red stain

of my hands

and rising up

weak

from within the ground
i would stumble away
   now the years go by
this lifetime too
pocketing
childhood effervescence
like crushed flowers
still i know
a sure sign
of something strong
when i see it
smell it
hear it
taste it
face it
on the air
again tonight
something strong moves
taking my thoughts away
stopping my heart
touching my spirit again
until my breath comes

as thunder before the wind

and the wind

then sings for me

breathing in

a homeland around me

bringing

a feast of dreams

to feed me

me

the one who comes

up out of silence

   it's up from silence

i've come to you

it's back to the inner earth

i'll go when i'm through

if the bones of your ears

can digest these words I say

then soon you will find

that i'm on my way

if i'm on my way

then so are you

for as long as untold stories

are always true

there is no way back

to zero for any of us

no matter what we do

    hold on tightly

to what you've already done

as the season of harvesting

has just begun

for every seed sown

under this earth's sun

the time for regeneration

has finally come

and the clan of the three

shall once more be made one

as the five who are buried

come back

to leave us

with our doing undone

    behold

within a primal scene of wonder

filled with rejuvenation and might

there moves

a swollen storm of thunder

birthing at the edge of night

behold

within this dream of darkness

broken by lightning

giving way to morning light

there comes a moment

of mutual surrender

where the ruling forces of nature

give way

to their own children's

ancestral birth right

behold

ancient light's gripping call

feel the pathway

touching all

behold!

solstice

    i have sat
in the presence of the queen
and made my request
to her attentive keepers
i have given gifts
of honeyed water
and restful sleep
in the valley of the northwind seekers
i was made to be a pole
in the medicine lodge
on the day
of the old god's returning
where i knelt and watched
as the faithful bowed down
at the end of their thirst for learning
    i travel now
on the shadow path
that rattles out
from throat of winter
following the fire in the east
as it gives way

to the humble promise
of a troubled beginner
who lives
to play a part
in the roundness of all things
curving back into an empty center
which neither gives nor asks
for what
i just can't remember.
   until i have
taken up in these hands
from beneath
the dark flowing water
the chalice of my heart
cradled in the arms
of the earth goddess's daughter
to gather in sweetness
my mother's milk
at the breast
of a cold stony boulder
where bathed
in the gray light
of this false dawn

her children stay young
while the world
grows ever older.
   i have reached
the northern limits
of every sea of thought
where each surface spray
freezes into feeling
then falls to shore
in the shape of dreams
filled with hidden meaning
that transform themselves
whenever i speak
into icy graves
opening at my feet
each a readied resting place
for the dying embers
of a smoldering faith
whose final flame was smothered
by my own disbelieving
   for yes
i have ridden with the king
in his search

for a true tomorrow

and i still stand

outside that ring

of those who would gain

through other's misfortunes and sorrow

my vision has suffered plainly

at the hands of time

still in my heart

i know what comes to mind

when again i see

that certain sign

etched

into someone else's eyes

so completely

for yes, i have sat

in the presence of the Queen

and her hand

touched my face

so sweetly.

sound of the living water

    twice

i awoke

after the dreaming

that was a sending

i was lying on my stomach

on a rock

in a cave

looking down

into a pool of water

the current flowed over

the stream flowed under

all life was connected

by the sound of the singing

which is the song of the water living

    in the pool

among the fishes

were many small carvings

each embedded in wax-like casings

golden yellow in their makings,

each with symbols on their bases,

all with melodies in the place of faces

that were speaking out in tongues

filled with the force of harmonious graces

which picked me up

and left me here

with these magical words

ringing in my ear.

   when i was a child

we played in the water

of an underground stream

while the earth above us

laughed like our mother,

and taught us new words to sing.

we knew what it was

to know who we are,

and what the future would bring

so we sang and we danced,

we loved all our life

for we lacked not a single thing.

our life was long,

our sorrows were short

until the day came

when we forgot to remember

what it feels like to hurt,

and then in the ways of thinking

sank a shaft right to the source

piercing the heart of our mother

now all that remains

is a pool of mud,

the taste of something

strong in our blood

and a heart that recalls

the way our life was

when this earth

was our one and only mother.

   may we never forget

at the water's edge

why what was clear

turned to red

and how quickly

our childhood fled

please forgive us now

our mother.

in the sending that came

through a dream that day

i know i heard

a familiar voice say

that there is an inner one
to be found
whose speech wells up
from that sovereign ground
whose strengths flow straight
from a spring of the older days
giving him visions clear and sound
which baptize me
as a child of that hidden realm
where every impulse
born of the other ways
allows me through his eyes
to bathe in your crystal gaze.
please tell me now, my mother,
before i was a child
you must have held us both close,
then you gave me this life
when i needed it most
and now you've sent to me
my own holy ghost
to help me fulfill
what must be this time's greatest boast:
that you are now

and forever my mother.

as long as the heavens

and stars are one

i shall remain your grateful son

and enter back

into the world again

on the red speech

of the ancient tongues of men

to fulfill the prophecies of the wind

to wash away with words

my mind's original sin

that i might return to you

hand in hand with my unborn twin

who has been watching and waiting

since forever

for this season of the sending to begin.

please welcome home

this child within

who though self-contained

still needs a friend

to share a drink of water

in order to mend

my wounded spirit

before the dark side
of your breath closes in
and brings to this thirst
an untimely end.
    please now my mother,
one drop of pure water please send
to my throat whose words
have grown so very dry and thin
before i forget where it is i've been
while all stretched out and waiting
for the rest of me to be born again
into this flatlander's body
that can no longer bend
to the will of spiral headed men.
    by the graceful signs
of unknown times
which sleep alone in my fingertips
i hereby call down to earth
heaven's glory
on my way to lay to rest
beside a streambed of ancient rhythms
filled with tenderness
that overflow to become the site

of tomorrow's dawning
bright with happiness,
for those who reach
the ocean's shore by morning
shall be baptized
with sunlight's celestial kiss
while i stay here
to keep these fires burning
with a steady wind
of perpetual emptiness.
yes, there is nothing
in the stars for me
except for emptiness
with all the fire i'll ever need
the cold's a welcomed guest.
in distant winters' dreams i fly
forever to leave this nest
for my heart knows
my home's in the sky
beyond all cleverness.
yes, there is nothing
in the stars for me
nothing but emptiness.

    why should i wait
for the rebirth of magic
so as to split the night
scattering before me
in every direction
galaxies of broken light
which shine on me
only as needed
in order to give out
all encompassing sight
except to see that
what i've really seeded
is a field of wrong
deeply embedded
into a world of right.
    there is i hear
a dark voice calling
off a cold wind that turns
on a hub of liquid life,
a spiral storm
whose speech is growing
by swallowing the weak
to feed its might.

awesome is a word

which holds no meaning

if you're being torn apart

and the old saying

that blood is thicker than water

is like a dream that's fading

when you're the thirsty one

who has no heart,

yet there is in every sense

a great awakening

once we step outside ourselves,

but who among us

can survive this hostile weather

that burns from within

while freezing from without.

so we practice

each time we awaken

dressing in our chosen fabric of life

a well-worn weave

not easily forsaken

even though the design

be stitched with sorrow and strife

for there is, i know,

no other enchantment

apart from dying alone

that can release us

from these prison castles

and return us

to the wildwood

of our childhood homes

where the sun still rises

with the morning

through arched columns of grass

and the dew begins each day

with a warning

of a time that just will not last

for the truth is

there is no justice

in any place whose fiction

is all too readily taken as fact

and the final seed of every flower

that will not blossom

always comes at the end

of a long and beautiful past.

   listen well to the names

that the night wind will be reciting

while i cradle them carefully

right from the start

know now

that the lords of eternity

are alive and inviting

your primal spirit to re-enter

through a doorway fashioned in the dark,

set straight the affairs

of this break-away culture,

stand still

inside a circle of stone,

wait there

for the strengths of original vision

to return and separate

the knower from the known,

that we might gather together

the drawstrings of a net of vapors

to once more capture

a breath of life to call our own

with which to begin that familiar portage

through the gateway passage

where every thought cuts us

just like a knife right to the bone.

i should have been born a seed
dormant in another place and time
then i would still be a thought asleep
in the back of the sky lord's mind
waiting to be reborn through a whisper
riding ebony-sculptured lips
then brought out again as a secret
from the deep lady's hips
who shall become another
to tell this child a lie
for all the brave
do at birth die.

run away

      what the mind thinks is but a shadow
of what the heart feels
    so run
run away from me my shadow
run straight into the mouth of the wind
take with you your arms, legs, and sorrows
take them all into the sky and bury them
    run
run away from me my shadow
hurry through both dark and light
travel across this bridge you've been building
go quickly now from my sight
vanish
beyond your own horizons into blindness
never to rise up with power and might
    run
run away from me my shadow
even though
i call to you from within
run, all the while your life is in motion
never knowing that running is the original sin

    play

play with your dreams my shadow

play as though you have nothing to lose

play until your hopes turn to dust my shadow

then play is what i'll do with you

or else you can stay

stay with me my shadow

    stay

that we may both grow strong and whole

stay with me my shadow

and i promise together

we will become easily old

(for what the mind thinks

is but a shadow of what the heart feels)

driving force

    how to say it?
so to speak of this
somewhere up a hill
along either side
of a broken down dream
woven in among
yellow brown leaves
shadows of light hide
moments of emptiness
and raindrops of silence.
    nine fold the wave
of the green man's muse
untold the days
of the night mare's brood
who claims the right
to pick and choose
when with each step you take
you stand to lose.
    colors left alone in the artist's eye
turn by themselves into memory
as time goes by

while words once drawn

from the poet's mind

fall easily from the tongue

and then forever into rhyme

these hands which give this world its feel

touch upon the surface

of all that is real

where beneath a taste

for life itself

there dwells the foundations

of something else.

   swim like otters

and jump like fish

from the middle

of the sub-strata streams

leap and play

then spin about

while waking

from a nighttime of dreams

the sunlight shows

the moonlight knows

what the mirror

can never tell:

the secret life

of who we are

once we stop

knowing ourselves

so well.

   an old man

took his traps

down to the sea

and all the fish

did seem to flee

as i was a child

they came to me

joyful

in their radiant idolatry.

   hunger is the driving force

the mouth to keep rivers

on their course

the gift to lead givers

to the source

of wisdom

pure and free.

   wind when it bites into the head

can shake the dreamer

from the dead

can wake the meaning

of what was said

from beneath the fragrant lips

of sleeping memory.

    in the gloaming of the twixt

there comes a moment

when the worlds do mix

where the half-formed tongues

of a forgotten earth still exist

singing from the depths of a dark abyss

with enchantment and harmony.

Aerion Cenote

    stay with me

earth's gravity said

to the moon

as the sun was passing by

i'll never leave

promised night time's shadow

to the morning

as a bright new dawn

filled the sky

come back

called out an empty river

to the ocean

leaving on low tide

this is it

cried the still heart

pointing

to an emptiness inside

it's too late

life alone within itself sighed

it's too late

for future generations to hide

it's too late

for anything but goodbye

    don't talk to me of starlight

with a twinkle in your eye

and i won't see life

as sunshine reflected

each night

when the moon is on the rise

know only

that tomorrow holds for us

all reason that will rhyme

with a season of flesh and blood

cradled in the essence of mankind

where one day we shall all

be born again together

from beneath the belly

of grandmother time

and what we are

will be given over

to a tenderness sublime

with the coming of a god-child

who is both forever yours

and will be always mine.

rapidly approaching lavender
heaven and earth are set aside
far horizons receding
reveal bloodlines of emptiness
that blindness can no longer hide
for deep inside shades of gray
that are gathering
behind eyes that can see
only black and white
wrapped in a blanket of stars
eternity's immortals sleep tonight
dreaming in an unknown language
like lost children
from some long forgotten genocide
who are seeking to reawaken
from within their memory
the vision to become
a being filled
with power and might
who together
with our ancestral offspring
give to all of those

who come within their sight
a blessing
which is fertility in motion
the rebirth
of our inherited right
to claim once more
personal sovereignty
over the outer reaches
of inner light
where the origins
of the fires of inner vision
have had the foresight to solidify
into a spectrum of tribal colors
from which truth may be identified
while on a journey to the surface
to be in allegiance
with the primordial alliance
of commodity, firmness and delight
which join together
in this forceful uprising
of twin currents
one of starlight blood
the other,

the love of life.
   so is it Celtic
or is it Shoshoni
who put the stars
above me
instead of below me
was it the Buddha
or was it the Christ
who opened my eyes
that i might close
them both twice
for i was Egyptian
before it was written
that language would be invented
as a healing prescription
to gather together
light out of dark
to call back from silence
the echo
of a still beating heart
which radiates with power
through the eye of the hawk
who carries on his shoulder

in a shape like a god
a watcher to keep guard
on our innermost thoughts
that our bodies might survive
this earth spirits assaults
as the moment comes quickly
for us to depart
this place of timed beginnings
and endless starts
which lead forever inward
but never down
like earthquake cracks
in an earthquake ground
      for i am
Egyptian
    Celtic
      and Shoshoni
  only the hawk
the sun-eyed god
and eternity know me
for i am
earth's echoing i
with silence

on either side

in exile

from the fruitful regions

of the bountiful sky

    where i am

a shaman

in suspension

for i am

a human reservoir

filling

with the flood waters

of another dimension

where i am

a willow bone framework

supporting

this tent of skin

for i am

a crystallized vortex

of unearthly wind

opening

directly into the source

of this vision

which burns within

where i am

a child

gently cradled

against the land

for i am

dark blood running

touching sand

where i am

a rough hollowed

wooden bowl

for i am

a metal hued

tight lipped soul

where i am

a wind drawn

naked eye

for i am

fixed sightless

on an empty sky,

    with half the world

as enemies

this civilization is filled

with fallen leaves

scattered thickly

across the earth

color is not

their only worth

for far beneath

the surface of what we see

ten thousand echoes gather

so patiently

every last one deserving to be first

each of them waiting

for you only

to give them birth

   for wherever

good luck and bad luck

come mixed together

the house of the lords

of the northern star

will stand forever

chief among

the winds at night

is this rush of air

that comes to court

bearing within it

a gift of prayer

for the newborn

of this world's

last twilight

   in the days

which lie ahead

no one knows

what it is

that should be said

it's only through seeking

this earth spirit's release

that our fragile dreams

will ever come

to rest in peace

after traveling

so recklessly

in the early morning light

there comes a time

of reckoning

just before wrong

turns to right

where between

the in breath

and out breath

of each mortal moment

of this heavenly life

there awaits unmoving

the edge of the blade

of the ceremonial knife

ready and willing

to sacrifice

the known

for the knowing

at any price

   shoulder to shoulder

the phantoms stand

wave upon wave

eroding

the summer shores

of this autumn land

where nation after nation

of winter people

arrive on command

emerging

with nothing more

than the sign of passage

in the palm of their hand

while asking

for their place at the table

that the feasting

might begin

with the taste

and the telling of stories

by the tongue of the wind

as gifts of memory

are given

again and again

in keeping with a doctrine

whose very existence depends

on the interrelated aspects

of a transdimensional clan

whose increase is timed

to coincide

with this world's

eventful end

as the first stages

of the age of stardust

overtake

the last days

of the season of man.

   nested deep inside

the heart of each of us

there is a feeling

we must come to trust

for if we are to spread

our wings and fly

first we must give up

all concept

of what it is to die

like caterpillars growing

from within a cocoon

we must face each day

working

to be awakened soon

for not much longer

can these feet survive

this earth bound pace

to which they're tied

before they feel

the need to climb

to transform

then to ride

beneath silken wings

that glide

on effervescent currents

and visionary tides

which give good cause

for the children of the froth

to rise

and greet again

with open eyes

the graceful return

of the titans of the skies.

   now some doubt it

so i've heard

but with no outward

sign to give

we must give our word

and hope that the sound of promise

travels with our voice

far enough to touch those

who like us

have no choice

but to follow

their own thoughts

back

to where it is

that we come from

to reach inside

and grab hold

of the inner one

who might otherwise

never overcome

this tangle of roots

which lie at the base

of the tongue

so as to speak

in a language

shared by everyone

in words composed

of syllables built

with fire and blood

each a flaming symbol

taken straight

from the heartland

of our native sun

where every life

is a glowing ember
waiting for the wind
and the word
to begin to become
a child ablaze
and burning again
in a world
which is forever fueled
with the rhythms
and incantations found
dwelling deep
within the boundaries
of this kingdom
of sight and sound
   for sound is to hearing
as hearing is to words
as words are to dreaming
as dreaming is to living
as living is to dying
each in a different light
gives another meaning
like stairs ascending
from a mute darkness

beyond all remembering

each step in the undertaking

becomes just one more small awakening.

   for from the top

the bottom is hidden

in minute misunderstandings

while from the bottom

the top is given an air

of being too demanding

all the while

the middle awaits

keeping each side

in constant embrace

by giving

the gift of centering

and so it is

that the journey begins

with one foot raised to fall

and brings about

a traveler's sense

of middle

beginnings

end and all

    come, dream with me at twilight

of beauty, heart, and home

let our spirits mix together

so that we will never be alone

as we travel along

the cracks of this world

where enchantments

come twice daily

in the hope

of sharing with us

this life

we've come to know

by giving a love

which flows quite freely.

    splendid in its isolation

tremendous in its desolation

unequalled in the enormity

of the entire situation

is the overshadowing revelation

that there is no one here at all

who can answer

without the slightest hesitation

their own primal mother's call.

    five times lately now
i've been born a man
seven times seven
before that
my breath has mixed
with the air of this land
three times each time
i've arrived at being
who i am
a fledgling fosterling
out to test the wind
if only to prove once again
that futility is the greatest sin.
with fire
falling back into darkness
on either side of me
blackness
would quickly overtake
all of what i see
if it were not
for these flaming tongues of fire
to light the path at my feet
while in a chant of dreams

hymns of eternity
rise up from restless sleep
hidden in the function
of articulated flowing speech
lies the formless faceless secrets
the greatest of which i keep
closest to the surface
though in all appearances
very deep
and if i were to say it
in just one word
that word
would have to be
now simply be.
if my memory
serves me well
there is little
left to tell`
more words
always count for less
when the message
is the silence
which follows all the rest

across a threshold of paradox

to become wedged

in the edge

of a vortex of silhouettes

that swirl unceasingly

about an open center

of nothing in particular

unless already hypnotized

into being personalized

as emptiness

and then reduced

again in size

as to be held captive

by the corners of our eyes

until that moment comes

when there can be no compromise

and all that we are

is easily recognized

among the sound and the vision

with which all our kinsman

have been blessed

as the source and the direction

of the universe itself

begins again to coalesce

into this cry of eons

which has gathered in our chest

and so i stand here still

with folded wings

across my breast

to protect my heart

until i can leave this nest

even though i know

i will be risking

at the very best

a long

and uncertain fall

which ends in a time

where i will still exist

tumbling head long

ever deeper

into an endless abyss

unless i can answer

unlike all the rest

my own hawk mama's call.

   when from within

a distant sound

like a storm of thunder

my absent parents'

voice is heard

recreating in an instant

that eternal urge

to join with them

in the elements

of their upper worlds

where this feeling of falling

naturally occurs

as the essence of being

moves outward

once more to merge

on singing wings

which turn the wind

to words

to lift up my body

with unknown verbs

that surge to speak

with action

during times of birth

of people and places

and each one's

own true worth.

    for yes there are feelings
that thoughts
just will not express
until after the myth
of their origins
has been laid to rest
beneath a marker
which contains this epitaph
that here none shall enter
and none shall pass
unless they can answer
each question
before it is asked
and thereby
climb a ladder
of riddle and rhyme
where every next rung
comes twice as fast
for the first one before it
is also always the last
and the language
of absolute nothingness

that the journey

is spoken in

tells all the futures

of every past

in just such a way

that the moment between

will last and last

while creating in the balance

a silence

which separates

the echo of this

from the echoing that

and gives to our feet

a feel for the path

which leads us to where

we've always been at

asleep and dreaming

long after the fact

that we've already awakened

sometime back.

    through many lives

i have been the same

though in each one known

by a different name

like broken links

of an unforged chain

i lie scattered and fallen

like autumn leaves

orphaned by a winter's rain

i wait only for this earth

my body to reclaim

and then the stars in heaven

shall my final extinction proclaim

as is the custom

with the ancients

by saying once

and once only

my original primal name

that i might come

at last to lie

at rest and in peace

beneath the banner

of the all seeing eye

which continues to forever fly

throughout the fruitful regions

of the bountiful sky.

falling

    in no hurry

    i do not wait

    for an unthinking thought

    to come

    by the time

    i get to where i am at

    there is nothing going on.

        so many leaves

    feel like falling

    with every little breeze

    that comes a calling

    still they have a job to do

    so out on a limb

    they stay

    until the tree they serve

    and the wind

    decide they're through.

starlord

    must we hasten
old age with sorrow
will it not come
of its own tomorrow
turning to fruit
our most youthful flower
releasing to seed
our most sovereign power
dissolving us again
like water into mist
as eternity's gateway veil
relentlessly lifts
to reveal heaven's fields
sown with an earthly bliss
that waits to be harvested
by a heart that captures
what these eyes will always miss

    please awake my heart
from beneath the hill
in the east

sleeping still

may deepening visions

come one by one

each morning

with the rising sun

gather around me

starlord of infinite sight

wash away

the shadows of the night

bathe me

in your glowing light

that i might see

the beauty

of this day

life has given me.

karmic pool

    there is nothing
spirit would not give
to those who
are want to steal
except perhaps
warm laughter
on smooth sunshine
or moonlight
bent across the window sill
    the parents
of our father's generation
took their turn
upon the wheel
building the foundations
of a fortress of wrong and right
that crumbles now
beneath the weight
of all that's real
    when i was young
i stayed inside
their house of silence

guarding what i feel

like all children

born alone

with no way to cry

i was given wounds

that can never heal

   to caress the shore

the swimmer rested

wave in hand

to ride your emotions

to the source

in the darkness

the ocean's voice demands

all life is connected

cries the water

running in

and out the sand

except for those

who are earth bound

and rooted

by a marriage of honor

to the blood

of the clan

and for them

there can be no peace

in their hearts

no way to understand

how to place their feet

upon a bridge of light

and thereby cross over

into the promise land

where no one

ever needs to focus

on the equality of being a man

for all those who go there

arrive without leaving

and take with them

no position

on which to make a stand.

bowsong

    the string was there
cutting the darkness
of a dream unbroken
when first that word
of this quest was spoken
releasing with power
the bowsong
whose strength in me
remains as a token
of the archer's arm
long after
his hand has opened
    many of my words
are pointed at nothing
they target that emptiness
from which all things grow
like arrows that have been
too long in the quiver
their meanings depend
on what you already know
    i will never be
a circle joiner
for i am a flatlander

straight and true

destined by my will

and the laws of nature

to carry the hunt forward

as i pass from view

    that one day

i must come to rest

on the ground is certain

soon after this flight

of feeling is through

even then

the quaking song of the bowstring

will from the inner earth rise up

and tell me what to do

    for yes there is a word

which lies behind every arrow

who has traveled the wind

on behalf of the bow

like a whisper riding

a wave revealing

the image can not help

but to grow and grow

until breaking the barrier

of a sound unspoken

that word comes screaming

down the string again
charging every fiber
in my being with leaving
by filling out my function
with the force of the flow
until the disappearing art
of inheriting motion
is all i have left
with which to show
that the archer's will
is once more intent on bending
as the voice of my instincts
end their sending
by saying soft and low
   "to swallow your loneliness
is the heart of an arrow
be on your way
now quickly, go."

out lined

    there could have been poetry this morning
a thoughtful emergence of sensitive words
yes, there could have been poetry this morning
a window to bridge between two worlds
    there might be poetry by noontime
standing full-face beneath the ark of the sun
there might be poetry in my mind
a simple way to leave my doing undone
    there should be poetry by evening
watching as darkness falls from the sky
yes, there should be poetry mixed with dreaming
moments of liquid emptiness gliding
from the heart to awaken the eye
    there will be poetry by midnight
sleeping in the stillness of unmeasured time
yes, there is always poetry at midnight
a mosaic of graceful intensity
rich in rhythm and rhyme,
a tapestry of starlit blackness
back stitched with silence
of the resourceful kind.

    there must be poetry in my living;
a pathway of memory skillfully outlined,
enduring words of deep understanding
fleshed out in feelings – sweet and sublime,
a pulsating language of vertical wisdom
unfolding with the greatest treasure
a seeker can find:
an ancient method of preserving in essence
a message that reason never defines,
the secret – a mystery of unbounded being
content now for the moment
to remain partially hidden
in these quiet spaces between the lines.
  yes,
        there could have been poetry this morning…

About the Author

Joseph Samuel Plum is a direct descendant of Welsh bards and Native American spirit. He lives in South Central Iowa within a group of trees where he composes and presents oral bardic poetry of original nature. He has been doing this for fifty years. This is his eighth book.

Books by Joseph S. Plum

RELICS
CONCENTRIC DEVOTION
LANDMASS AND OTHER POEMS
STAR SIGHT GATHERING
WHERE RISING VOICES GROW
HUMAN LANDSCAPE
NOBLE REMNANTS
BOOK OF SHADOWS
OLD PATH

www.JoePlum.com

www.ingramcontent.com/pod-product-compliance
Lightning Source LLC
Chambersburg PA
CBHW051700090426
42736CB00013B/2458